D0573010

THE SCOTTSBORO BOYS

Essential Events

THE SCOTTSBORO
BOYS

BY DAVID CATES

Content Consultant
James A. Miller
Professor of English and American Studies
The George Washington University

Publishing Company

CREDITS

Published by ABDO Publishing Company, PO Box 398166,
Minneapolis, MN 55439. Copyright © 2012 by Abdo Consulting
Group, Inc. International copyrights reserved in all countries.
No part of this book may be reproduced in any form without
written permission from the publisher. The Essential Library™
is a trademark and logo of ABDO Publishing Company.

Printed in the United States of America,
North Mankato, Minnesota
092011
012012

Editor: Mari Kesselring and Lisa Owens
Copy Editor: Mary Jo Plutt
Cover Design: Marie Tupy
Interior Design and Production: Kazuko Collins

Library of Congress Cataloging-in-Publication Data
Cates, David, 1963-
  The Scottsboro boys / by David Cates.
      p. cm. -- (Essential events)
  Includes bibliographical references.
  ISBN 978-1-61783-310-6
  1. Scottsboro Trial, Scottsboro, Ala., 1931--Juvenile literature.
2. Trials (Rape)--Alabama--Scottsboro--Juvenile literature. 3.
African Americans--Civil rights--History--Juvenile literature. 4.
Trial and arbitral proceedings--Juvenile literature. I. Title.
  KF224.S34C38 2012
  345.761'9502523--dc23
                                                  2011036128

TABLE OF CONTENTS

The Scottsboro case defendants were escorted into the courthouse in Decatur, Alabama, by members of the US National Guard.

SEGREGATION AND JIM CROW

It was April 9, 1931, in Scottsboro, Alabama. Nine young men charged with rape, ranging in ages from 13 to 19, stood at the mercy of the court. The jury wasted no time in handing down the sentences for eight of the young men: death in the electric chair. The trial of the remaining young man, a 13-year-old, was rendered a mistrial because the jury could not decide between giving the boy life in prison or a death sentence.

When the trial started on April 6, it was a festive day in Scottsboro—Fair Day. On this day, farmers and others set up shop in the town square to sell their produce and goods. As they worked, they caught up on the latest news and gossip. The weather was nice. The square was very crowded with approximately five times the number of cars on the street as usual. Some estimated the crowd to be almost three times the town's population of 3,500.

Fair Day was always popular, but many people had traveled from miles away for the trial of the young men, who were soon to become known as the "Scottsboro Boys. People from the local community and beyond waited for the young men to be brought to justice. For most people,

"Boys"

During slavery and under segregation in the South, many white men referred to African American men as "boys" to make them feel inferior. At thirteen, the youngest of the Scottsboro Boys could technically be considered boys and not men. However, given that eight of the nine accused were tried as adults, the use of the term "boy" in the media can be interpreted as a part of the racist tradition of putting down African American men. At the same time, defenders of the Scottsboro Boys used the term to emphasize the defendant's youth and innocence, trying to gain sympathy for them.

Guilty of What?

The presumption of guilt by many white southerners and the southern press was no surprise to anyone, much less the nine young men on trial. To many in the south, the fact that they were even present on the same train as the white women was reason enough for the death sentence. During the trials, Alabama Congressman George Huddleston stated that he did not "care whether the boys were innocent or guilty. They were found riding on the same freight car with two white women, and that's enough for me. . . . I'm in favor of the boys being executed just as quickly as possible!"[3] While this statement is shocking today, it was not out of the ordinary for its place and time.

there was little question of their innocence. Due to the color of their skin, the white public and Alabama newspapers had already judged the young men—guilty.

The nine men had been arrested two weeks earlier. On the day of the arrests, a Scottsboro newspaper showed its prejudice in its headline, "Nine Negro Men Rape Two White Girls."[1] That same day, the Huntsville, Alabama, newspaper featured a front page article claiming that the nine had committed "one of the most brutal attacks in the history of the Tennessee Valley."[2] As the trials progressed, the southern press would continue to assert similar claims of the defendants' guilt. However, there was no concrete evidence that tied the defendants to the crime. In fact, there was nearly no evidence that the rapes occurred at all.

Racism in the United States

During this time, much of the United States, especially the south, held racist attitudes toward African Americans. Under law, African-American citizens and other people of color did not have the same rights as white citizens.

After the American Civil War (1861–1865), the south was in ruins economically and socially. The economic system of the south had been supported by slave labor. In 1865, the Thirteenth Amendment to the Constitution of the United States officially abolished the institution of slavery. Now, slaves were legally free. However, many white people in the south were unhappy with the results of the Civil War. They did not want African Americans to be free. Many held racist beliefs about African Americans and considered them inferior to white people.

With the end of slavery, the southern economy suddenly was without the free slave labor it had long depended upon for its economic prosperity and independence. The southern whites rushed to put into place a system that kept the freed slaves disempowered and beholden to white southerners.

Meanwhile, more federal laws that increased the rights of African Americans were passed. The Fourteenth Amendment granted full citizenship to black men in 1868. In 1870, the Fifteenth Amendment gave black men voting rights as well. The Civil Rights Act of 1875 declared that there should be no discrimination of blacks in public facilities.

Although these laws were great improvements, they meant little to the everyday experience of blacks in the south. African-American

The Ku Klux Klan

The racist group Ku Klux Klan (KKK) was formed as a white-supremacist group in Pulaski, Tennessee, in 1866. The KKK worked outside the legal system to uphold the race divisions they saw as essential to southern culture by terrorizing and intimidating blacks. African Americans who were involved in activities such as voting, running for office, or refusing to work for whites often found themselves the target of KKK violence. The KKK was notorious for its brutality. Its members were known to lynch, whip, brand, rape, and murder their victims.

The Scottsboro case was no exception. E. L. Lewis was a witness for the defense. As he was giving testimony that conflicted with that of the two white women, his house was burned to the ground. Not long after he testified, Lewis was found dead. He had been poisoned. A Scottsboro newspaper reported on the Klan's influence on the trial:

Ku Klux Klan threats, both officially from the organization and from individual members, have been received by defense witnesses and their lawyers. Already in Jackson county [Scottsboro], a reign of terror against the Negro witnesses who testified for the defense on the exclusion of Negroes from juries, and two have been terrorized into signing repudiations of their testimony.[4]

rights were still limited under the new laws. The Supreme Court ruled that, in order to vote, African Americans had to meet certain criteria. Blacks wanting to register to vote were told they had to be able to read or correctly answer complex questions. White men, on the other hand, were allowed to vote without passing any of these tests. Additionally, because many people were prejudiced against African Americans and did not believe they should be allowed to vote, African Americans who did try to vote often risked retaliation. They could be fired from their jobs, beaten, or even killed if they dared to show up at the polls on voting day.

Another way for whites to maintain social control through terror was lynching. The lynching of people of color in the United States has a long history. In Alabama alone, from 1882 to 1968, 299 African Americans were lynched. The total of African Americans lynched in the entire United States for the same time period was 3,446. The threat of death to blacks who stood up for their rights was very real. It kept many of them from speaking out against their unfair treatment because they were afraid of what could happen.

JIM CROW LAWS

Beginning in 1877, southern states adopted what were called Jim Crow laws. These laws kept whites and people of color segregated and enforced the idea that African Americans were second-class citizens. African Americans had to use restaurants, restrooms, and even drinking fountains that were separate from the ones whites used. Additionally, in the south, local governments passed what would come to be known as black codes. These were laws that banned blacks from activities such as serving on juries, renting or owning land, carrying arms, and even reading, among others.

The Scottsboro Boys were entrenched in this atmosphere of racism, segregation, and discrimination. Accused of heinous crimes, imprisoned, tried, and sentenced to death, the young men were in a life or death struggle against a system filled with ignorance and race hatred. —

Reconstruction

After the Civil War, much of the south was suffering from the destruction of the war. The Reconstruction period took place from the end of the Civil War in 1865 to 1877. This was when the last northern troops withdrew from the south. The US government worked to rebuild the south. During this time, blacks saw some improvement in the laws that governed them. However, laws called black codes passed by white Reconstruction governments left southern blacks in much the same political and social position as they held during slavery.

A water cooler labeled "colored" in Oklahoma City, Oklahoma, illustrates the Jim Crow laws.

A boy steals a ride on a train during the Depression.

THE TERRIBLE JOURNEY
BEGINS

*I*n Chattanooga, Tennessee, the morning of March 25, 1931, was clear but chilly. Four young African-American men hopped on a freight train. The four were friends—18-year-old Haywood Patterson, 13-year-old Eugene Williams, and 19-year-old Andy Wright and his 13-year-old brother, Leroy "Roy" Wright. This was Roy's first trip away from home. They were riding as far as Memphis, Tennessee, each hoping to find work. The train's course would make a short dip down into Alabama before heading back through Tennessee.

The train had other riders, black and white. Many of the riders were heading to other cities in hope of finding work. This practice was called hoboing. It was technically illegal because riders did not pay for tickets. During the economic hard times of the early 1930s, the law was not strictly enforced.

THE CONFRONTATION

As Patterson later recalled it, the ride was uneventful at first. As the train emerged from a tunnel on Lookout Mountain in Tennessee, the four friends were hanging from the side of a tank car when a group of young white men walked along the top of the car. One of the white men stepped on Patterson's hand. Though painful, Patterson said nothing about the injury.

In the south, during the 1930s and long before, African Americans knew that challenging a white person, even if the white person was clearly in the wrong, could be dangerous or even deadly. So Patterson kept his mouth shut.

When the same white teen stepped on his hand again, Patterson spoke up. He told the white teen to ask when he wanted to get by, and Patterson would gladly let him pass.

The white teen got angry. He reportedly responded, "I don't ask you when I want by. . . . This is a white man's train. . . . All you black bastards better get off!"[1]

The young white men moved on. When the train stopped in Stevenson, Alabama, other African-American

---

Reasons for Hoboing

During the Great Depression (1929–1940), there were many thousands of people out of work and on the move—so many that the police often looked the other way when it came to enforcing laws regarding hoboing. One of the Scottsboro Boys, Clarence Norris, explained:

> Funny thing, at one time they were arresting people for being hoboes and jailing them for thirty days or something like that. After a while there was just too many of us and they realized that feeding all these people was just too much, so they just stopped bothering us.[2]

Many of the jobless who could not find work locally would use the rail system to travel to other towns or cities, in hopes of gaining employment there. Norris explained:

> As hoboes, we was like anyone else looking for work, except we chose to travel by train from city to city by stealing a ride. . . . Traveling this way you could cover eighty or a hundred miles in a fairly short period of time, and it sure beats walking. I'll tell you something else, you'd see just as many whites out there hoboing as there were blacks.[3]

men, who were also hoboing, joined Patterson's group. Patterson told the newcomers about the incident. They agreed to band together if the whites started harassing them again.

Shortly after the train pulled away from Stevenson, the young white men began their harassment again, this time from another train car. Patterson and ten others responded with fists. The white teens lost the fight and all but one either jumped or were thrown off the train. The exception was Orville Gilley, who was pulled up from where he was hanging from the side of a gondola car. Patterson's group did not eject Gilley from the train because they feared the train had gained too much speed to throw him off safely.

The young men who had joined Patterson and his friends then dispersed to other parts of the train. By the time the train stopped again, the young men were spread throughout the train, alone or in small groups.

Meanwhile, the whites who had been thrown from the train were angry. The group made their way back to the train station in Stevenson. There, they told the stationmaster that they had been thrown from the train by a group of African Americans and that

Orville Gilley was the only white teen in the fight who avoided being thrown from the train.

they wanted to press charges. The legality of whether the young white men should have been on the train in the first place was never called into question.

The Arrests

When the county sheriff, M. L. Wann, was notified of the fight on the train, he alerted a deputy near the next town along the train's path—Paint Rock, Alabama. The deputy was instructed to round up every white man with a gun he could find. When the train stopped at the Paint Rock station, the deputy was to pull every African-American man off the train and take him into custody. When the train stopped in Paint Rock, it was met by dozens of white men armed with pistols, rifles, and shotguns. They captured nine African-American men: Patterson, Williams, Olen Montgomery, Clarence Norris, Ozie Powell, Willie Roberson, Charles Weems, and the two Wright brothers. Others had hidden or escaped.

The nine were tied together with a thick rope and loaded onto a flatbed truck. When Patterson asked about the crime they were accused of committing, he was told the charges were assault and attempted murder. They were driven some 25 miles (40 km) away to Scottsboro, where they were jailed.

A New Accusation

Two young white women, Ruby Bates and Victoria Price, did not draw immediate attention. They had also been hoboing on the train, dressed in men's overalls. However, 20 minutes after the train stopped, one of the women either volunteered or answered affirmatively that the young black men had raped her and the other woman.

Hours later, the nine young men were taken from their cells and lined up against the wall. Bates and Price were brought before them. Wann asked the women which of the men had raped them. Price pointed to six of the young men. A guard then said, "If those six had Miss Price, it stands to reason that the others had Miss Bates."[4]

One of the nine, Clarence Norris, cried out, "Woman, you're telling a lie, you ain't never seen me before."[5] A guard responded with his bayonet, slashing Norris' hand to the bone, yelling, "You know damn well how to talk about white women!"[6]

For the nine men standing against the wall, the severity of the situation began to sink in. Still, they never could have imagined what would happen next. ⌐

Witness Victoria Price took the stand during the Scottsboro trials. Price and Ruby Bates claimed the African Americans on the train had raped them.

More than 10,000 people crowded the courthouse square in Scottsboro, Alabama, for the opening trials of the Scottsboro Boys' case.

THE TRIAL

mmediately after the nine African-American young men were jailed in Scottsboro, a crowd of several hundred people, some with guns, gathered outside the jail. The people yelled to Sheriff Wann to let the prisoners out so justice could be done by the mob. When Wann did not comply, the people of the mob threatened to enter the jail and take the boys out themselves. Wann called Alabama Governor Benjamin Meeks Miller for help. National Guard troops were dispatched to protect the young men from the mob. The young men were also moved to a more secure jail in nearby Gadsden, Alabama, where they awaited their trial.

THE PROSECUTION AND THE DEFENSE

The first day of trials was April 6, 1931. The courtroom was full. The jury pool consisted of 100 white men between the ages of 21 and 65. Alabama law did not expressly forbid blacks from serving on a jury, but cultural codes prevented it. Patterson said that he had only seen two African Americans in all of Scottsboro. He described the courtroom as "one big smiling white face."[1]

The defendants needed legal counsel. Lawyer Stephen Roddy of Chattanooga was sent to help the young men in court. He was not licensed to practice law in Alabama and was a heavy drinker. He was so drunk on the first morning of the trial that, according to a member of the prosecution team, "he could scarcely walk straight."[2]

After a short conversation with Judge A. E. Hawkins, it became apparent that Roddy was there only to assist, not lead the defense. Instead, Milo Moody, a local lawyer, offered to join the defense team. Moody was nearly 70 years old. He was described by those who knew him as "an ancient Scottsboro lawyer of low type and rare practice."[3] Others called him "a doddering, extremely unreliable, senile individual who is losing whatever ability he once had."[4] The defense team consulted the young men for only 30 minutes prior to their trial.

"I didn't know what a lawyer was supposed to be, but I knew this one was no good for us. He had liquor on his breath and he was as scared as we were. When we got into the courtroom and the judge asked him if he was our lawyer, the man said, 'Not exactly.'"[5]

—*Norris*

The prosecution pushed to have the accused prosecuted in groups, first trying Weems, Norris, and Roy Wright together. Then the court would try Patterson, followed by the trial of Montgomery, Powell, Roberson, Williams, and Andy Wright. Here Roddy raised his only objection. He said that Roy Wright and Williams were both under 16 and therefore should be tried in juvenile court. It was decided that Roy Wright would be tried on his own following the other three trials. But because the court had some doubt over Williams's real age, Williams would be tried as an adult.

The Trial Begins

The trial of Weems and Norris was first. The first witness, Victoria Price, was called to the stand. She testified that in Chattanooga she and Bates had hopped a train headed for Huntsville, Alabama. She said they were riding in a gondola car with seven white boys when 12 black boys jumped into the car from an adjacent boxcar. One of the black boys, who she identified as Weems, was waving a .45 pistol. The black boys ordered the white boys to jump off the moving train, which they did. Price then claimed that Norris tore off her clothes and raped her while Weems held a knife to her throat and others held her legs.

On cross-examination, Price said that she and Bates had gone to Chattanooga on March 24 looking for work. They stayed one night at the house of

"The first lawyer we had in Scottsboro was some little white guy out of Tennessee . . . Stephen Roddy. We had never seen him until the day we were supposed to go on trial. He got us all in a side room in the court-house and told us that some little group in Tennessee sent him down to Alabama to defend us. He added, 'it was possible to save some of your lives if you plead guilty to all the charges. . . .' We told him we wasn't going to plead guilty to anything which we didn't do."[6]

—*Norris*

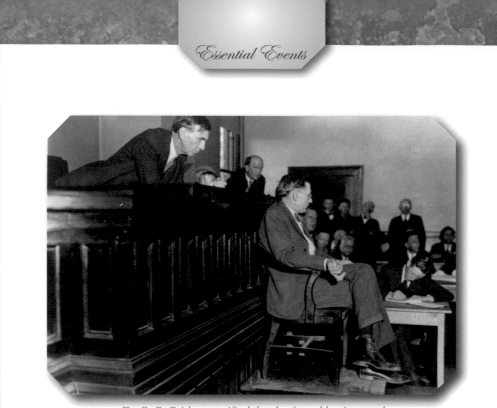

Dr. R. R. Bridges testified that he found bruises and minor scratches on Price after the alleged attack. Judge James E. Horton leaned in to hear the testimony.

Mrs. Callie Brochie, a friend of Price's. Unsuccessful in their attempt to find work, Price and Bates boarded a train in Chattanooga on March 25, hoping to return to Huntsville, Alabama.

Price added that six of the black boys raped her, and six others (three of whom, she said, escaped before capture) raped Bates. She also said that at one point she was hit in the head with the butt of a gun. Price testified that after the rapes, the men told her and Bates "they were going to take us north and make us their women or kill us one."[7]

The next to testify were the two doctors who examined Price and Bates less than two hours after the alleged rapes. Dr. R. R. Bridges reported that Price did not seem very upset. He said that she had some small bruises and a short scrape on one arm. He did find sperm in her vagina, but the sperm was nonmotile, meaning it was unmoving, dead. Living sperm can survive inside a woman's body for approximately five days. Dr. H. M. Lynch affirmed Dr. Bridges findings.

The trial continued the next day with Bates testifying. She told much the same story that Price had told. She claimed that she was raped by six of the boys and a knife was held to her throat. The prosecution closed with the testimonies of three men who claimed to witness the violence of the young men against both the young white men and the women.

The Defense Calls . . .

The defense called only two witnesses, the defendants, Weems and Norris. Weems was first. On the stand Weems said that he had been threatened by Patterson, who had a gun, to "[come] on and help me get the white boys off."[8] Weems denied that he had anything to do with the white girls and said he had not even seen them until they unloaded in Paint Rock. On cross-examination, Weems testified he had seen Norris, Powell, Roberson, and Montgomery on the gondola car with the white boys, but saw nothing done to the girls.

Norris was next on the stand. The lack of preparation on the part of the defense attorneys revealed itself in drastic ways as Norris's story began falling apart. He said Patterson had said he was "going to have something to do with them white girls" after throwing the white boys off the train. During cross-examination,

---

Testifying against Each Other

Although the accused is considered innocent until proven guilty by law, this did not hold true for the Scottsboro Boys. A number of tactics were used to coerce the boys into testifying against each other.

Roy Wright, age 13 at the time of his arrest, was encouraged to testify against Patterson. When Roy refused, the trial was called to recess. Roy remembered:

Then the trial stopped awhile and the deputy sheriff beckoned me to come out into another room—the room back of the place where the judge was sitting—and I went. They whipped me and it seemed like they was going to kill me. All the time they kept saying, 'Now will you tell?' and finally it seemed like I couldn't stand no more and I said yes. Then I went back into the courtroom and they put me up on the chair in front of the judge and began asking a lot of questions, and I said I had seen Charlie Weems and Clarence Norris with the white girls.[9]

Norris continued to unwind, saying "I seen every one of them have something to do with those girls. . . . They all raped her, every one of them."[10]

The defense team made no closing arguments. Judge Hawkins instructed the jury and sent them off for deliberations.

PATTERSON'S TRIAL

As Weems's and Norris's fates were decided, the next trial was set into motion. Another all-white jury was seated, and the trial of Patterson began. Shortly after it started, Patterson's trial was paused. The jury for the Weems and Norris trial had come to a decision. Weems and Norris were found guilty of rape and sentenced to death. The courtroom erupted in cheers and celebration. Patterson's jury had been removed to a room only 20 feet (6 m) from the courtroom. There was an open window above the door, leaving little doubt that Patterson's jury heard the commotion in the court when the decision was read.

When Patterson's trial resumed, his defense council called for a mistrial, stating that Patterson's jury had been influenced by the rejoicing at the guilty verdict. The request was denied.

During Patterson's trial, and for the remaining trials, Price's testimony became more colorful and detailed. She had the court laughing one moment and horrified the next. Dr. Lynch had been excused from the trial, but Dr. Bridges continued to testify. His testimony became more partial and damaging to the defense.

> "I was convicted in [the jury's] minds before I went on trial. . . . All that spoke for me on that witness stand was my black skin—which didn't do so good."[11]
>
> —*Patterson*

Patterson himself also complicated the trial by giving conflicting testimony. At one point, he claimed to have seen five of the boys rape Price and Bates. Then Patterson recanted, saying that he had no knowledge of the girls on the train. Roy Wright, testifying in Patterson's case, said that he had seen all but himself and his brother, Patterson, and Williams (the four from Chattanooga) raping the women.

THE POWELL, WILLIAMS, ROBERSON, MONTGOMERY, AND ANDY WRIGHT TRIAL

Patterson's trial finished late in the morning on April 8. The jury was sent out to deliberate, and the trial of Powell, Williams, Roberson, Montgomery, and Andy Wright began. Price again took the stand and continued to embellish her testimony. She now claimed she had heard seven gunshots from the gondola, having previously claimed she heard one or two.

Before lunch, Patterson's jury came in with a verdict. The jury found Patterson guilty of rape. His sentence was death in the electric chair.

When the trial resumed after lunch, the five defendants all pled their innocence. Roberson was on the way to Memphis to find treatment for his severe syphilis. His genitals were so swollen it was impossible for him to have sexual intercourse, willing or not. Montgomery was on his way to Memphis to get new eyeglasses. He was practically blind in one eye and could not see well from the other. The others denied any knowledge of the women on the train. The third day of trials ended with the jury for the five leaving for deliberation.

Roy Wright Trial

By 9:00 a.m., April 9, the fourth day of the trials, the jury for the five young men reported they had come to a decision—all five defendants were found guilty of rape and sentenced to death.

The Verdict

On April 9, 1931, Judge Hawkins read the sentences for five of the defendants. He had tears in his eyes as he read the verdict. The young men were to be electrocuted on July 10, 1931.

The jury for Roy Wright continued deliberating into the afternoon. Finally, they sent a message to Judge Hawkins—the jury was deadlocked. A jury must come to a unanimous decision for the trial to proceed. Even though they were instructed not to consider the death penalty for Roy, some on the jury demanded that he die in the electric chair. Others on the jury wanted to sentence him to life in prison. The judge had no alternative but to call a mistrial.

At the end of the four days of court proceedings, Roy's fate still hung in the balance. The other eight boys had been sentenced to death in the electric chair. They were taken to Kilby Prison near Montgomery, Alabama, to await their end.

SCOTTSBORO, ALA., APRIL 2, 1931

ON CHARGES OF RAI

LEGED NEGRO ATTACKERS AND THEIR VICTI

...ured above are the nine
...oes indicted on a charge
...ping two white girls af-
...they had thrown the
... boy companions of
... girls off a Southern
...ht train between Stev-
... and Scottsboro Wed-
...ay of last week. In the
...o the negroes are seen
...d by soldiers with
...c rifles and riot

A Scottsboro newspaper reports on the results of the trial.

SCOTTSBORO BOYS MUST NOT DIE!

MASS SCOTTSBORO DEFENSE MEETING

At St. Mark's M. E. Church

137th Street and St. Nicholas Avenue

Friday Eve., April 14th, 8 P. M.

Protest the infamous death verdict rendered by an all-white jury at Decatur, Alabama against HAYWOOD PATTERSON

The Meeting will be addressed by:

Mrs. JANIE PATTERSON, mother of Haywood Patterson, victim of the lynch verdict; SAMUEL LEIBOWITZ, chief coun-l for the defense; JOSEPH BRODSKY, defense counse

*Some people were outraged by the guilty verdicts.
They protested the decision.*

SUPPORT FOR THE BOYS

Although the Scottsboro courtroom had been filled with people who seemed certain of the boys' guilt, many people around the United States soon began questioning the court's decision. They felt the young men had been unfairly accused and sentenced. Many groups and organizations began speaking out in their favor.

In the courtroom during the trial, there had been two representatives from the Communist Party of the United States of America (CPUSA). The representatives were sending reports of the trial to party headquarters in New York. During the trial, the CPUSA had written articles disparaging what they termed "a legal lynching" of the young men in the Alabama court.[1] Three weeks after the trial, the CPUSA held its first of many demonstrations for the Scottsboro Boys. Approximately 1,500 demonstrators walked through the streets of Harlem, holding signs and chanting for their release. Police broke up the demonstration.

THE CPUSA's INTEREST IN THE CASE

The Scottsboro Boys caught the attention of the CPUSA as the party was looking to become more relevant in national politics during the 1930s. In 1931, the Great Depression was in full swing, and tens of thousands were without work. The financial system of the United States and much of the world seemed to be failing. Some wondered if the Depression spelled the end of capitalism. The CPUSA saw this as a time to unite the workers of the United States and initiate a Communist revolution. To do so, they needed the support of all workers, men and women, black and white.

The CPUSA saw the struggles of the southern black as an ongoing fight against slavery. Even though the former slaves were legally free according to the constitution, many in the south still lived in a system that kept them terrified and poor. The plantation system of the slaveholding south had transitioned into a sharecropping system that still essentially enslaved the poor.

The CPUSA saw the Scottsboro case

Sharecropping

The fall of the slaveholding south did not necessarily mean freedom for blacks. A system was quickly put into place to legally keep southern blacks enslaved. Southern economies relied upon agriculture to survive. Before the Industrial Revolution, and even after, humans were needed to work the fields. In the south, slaves had done this work. After the slaves were freed, the white landowners instituted a farming system to ensure that the freed slaves would be forced to work the land. It was called sharecropping.

Sharecropping is a system under which someone farms a section of a landowner's land for a share of the crops. This share can come in the form of food or money. However, many southern sharecroppers' supplies had to be purchased at the landowner's company store. The sharecropper would run a tab at the company store. When it came time to pay the bill, if the sharecropper could not pay, he or she would have to sign on for another year of sharecropping. This process kept free blacks working the land for white landowners year after year.

as a chance to draw southern blacks into its cause. Without black support, the CPUSA believed it had little hope for causing a revolution that would include the south and, therefore, the whole of the United States. The legal arm of the CPUSA, the International Legal Defense (ILD), began trying to convince the boys to appeal the court's ruling and let the ILD defend them in court. The ILD had been gathering support from across the country for the young men, asking supporters to send letters and other tokens. Many of these supporters were outraged by the first trial and wanted them to be retried in higher court.

Showing Support

One aspect of the CPUSA's involvement was its focus on the rights of workers, regardless of race. Party members, many of them white, were encouraged to send their support to the Scottsboro Boys. Many of the young men, including Patterson, were surprised by this response. Patterson explained, "Mail from white people was confusing to me. All my life I was untrusting of them. Now their kind words and presents was more light than we got through the bars of the windows."[2]

The NAACP

The National Association for the Advancement of Colored People (NAACP) was also interested in the Scottsboro case. They were late with their support, however. They were concerned the evidence against the boys was overwhelming and did not want

Protesters at a Communist rally in New York City in 1932 held signs calling for the release of the Scottsboro Boys.

to be seen as protectors of rapists. The NAACP also worried that the CPUSA was using the young men to further the Communist cause. The NAACP felt bringing in outsiders would prejudice the court against the defendants and limit their chances for a fair trial.

Choosing Representation

The young men had trouble deciding who would represent them in their appeals. Their decisions varied—some chose the ILD, some the NAACP.

Some changed their minds. It was at this point that the ILD realized they were trying to convince the wrong people. They began talking to the defendants' mothers.

Even though the mothers were warned to refuse aid from the ILD—by the clergy, the NAACP, and many others—they decided to stick with the ILD. One reason for the mothers' choice was the difference in the way they were treated by the ILD and the NAACP.

The ILD not only asked to defend their sons, but also for the mothers' participation in bringing international attention to the case. Ada Wright, mother of Roy and Andy Wright, wrote that the ILD was the only organization that had "discussed the case with them, and asked [for the mothers'] support."[3] In the fall of 1931, the ILD took five of the mothers on a nationwide tour to spread the word about the case and raise money for the defense. The following year, Ada Wright accompanied the ILD national

"I had never met white men like them before. These men brought the first kind words from the outside world since we had been arrested."[4]

—Norris, commenting on the attitudes of the ILD lawyers

secretary on a six-month tour that included stops in 13 different countries. On this tour, she spoke of the plight of her sons and the other Scottsboro Boys.

The NAACP interacted with the families in a wholly different way. They did not confer with the mothers. They merely wanted the mothers to give permission for the NAACP to represent the young men. When the parents refused or asked for time to think on the decision, one NAACP official referred to them in private as ignorant and unrefined. This attitude was not unnoticed by the parents.

"[W]hile the ILD was willing to take on a case in the southern states like ours . . . the NAACP was concerned about the legal cost of such a strategy, the constant harassment this would surely invoke for its membership to say nothing about the dangers it felt existed in being associated with national and international Communist and socialist entities."[6]

—*Norris*

Mamie Williams, mother of Eugene Williams, explained, "We are not too ignorant to know a bunch of liars and fakers when we meet up with them, and not too ignorant to know that if we let the NAACP look after our boys, that they will die."[5]

On June 22, 1931, Judge Hawkins postponed the July 10 execution date. The stage was set for the ILD attorneys, Joseph Brodsky and George Chamlee, to argue the case before the Alabama Supreme Court.

Mrs. Montgomery, Mrs. Williams, Mrs. Patterson, Mrs. Norris, and Mrs. Powell rode in a protest to demand the release of their sons.

Leading the fight to convict the Scottsboro Boys were Attorney General
Thomas E. Knight Jr., left, and Assistant Attorney General Thomas Lawson.

THE SUPREME COURT

The proceedings in the Alabama Supreme
Court began on January 21, 1932. Once
again, the odds were not in the Scottsboro Boys'
favor. Alabama had received numerous pleas to
free the young men, but many of these pleas were

antagonistic, implying that racist, mob-mentality ruled in Alabama. The court was not pleased. The people in Alabama were also suspicious of the ILD lawyers, especially Brodsky, because he was from New York and considered an outside agitator. These were not the only things that may have negatively influenced the ILD's case. Arguing the case for the state was the attorney general of Alabama, Thomas E. Knight Jr., whose father sat on the Alabama Supreme Court.

The court reached its decision on March 25, upholding the convictions of seven of the boys on death row. Eugene Williams, whose age was contested, would be retried in a juvenile court. The ILD argued that the trial should have been conducted in another city because of the negative publicity surrounding the case. To this, Judge Thomas E. Knight Sr. wrote:

The Appeals Process

When a defendant is found guilty, he or she can appeal the verdict or the sentence to a higher court. The defense must show that a legal error was made during the trial in order for the higher court to overturn the sentence or verdict. The higher court can order the case be retried. If the higher court does not overturn the verdict, the defendant can appeal the case to the US Supreme Court. The Supreme Court chooses the cases it hears; it usually chooses cases that concern an important legal or constitutional principle. A US Supreme Court decision is final.

The character of the crime was such as to arouse the indignation of the people, not only in Jackson and the adjoining counties, but every where where womanhood is revered, and the sanctity of their persons is respected. . . . The record of the facts . . . does not disclose a single act done by the populace to show a disposition to take the law into its own hand. . . . To the contrary, considering the nature of the crime and its revolting features, the people seem to have conducted themselves with a commendable spirit and a desire to let the law take its due course.[1]

THE US SUPREME COURT

An appeal was then made on behalf of the young

Moore v. Dempsey

Nine years before the Scottsboro case, the Supreme Court had ruled on a very similar case—*Moore v. Dempsey*. In this case, which also took place in the south, several African Americans were charged with murdering five white men during a race riot on September 30, 1923. A lynch mob formed, but Federal troops intervened before the defendants could be killed. The defendants were brought to trial on November 3 and appointed legal counsel by the court. The jury was 12 white men. As in Scottsboro, the courtroom was surrounded by a mob of whites.

In his ruling, Supreme Court Justice Holmes commented that the trial took only 45 minutes and the jury returned its guilty verdict, first-degree murder, in only a few minutes. Holmes stated that acquittal was never an option because if a juror voted for acquittal he would be run out of town and any defendant that was acquitted would be taken by the mob.

As would happen in the Scottsboro case, the Supreme Court found that in the case of *Moore v. Dempsey* the rights guaranteed to the defendants by the Fourteenth Amendment were violated.

men to the Supreme Court of the United States. On October 10, 1932, ILD attorney Walter Pollak presented the case to the Supreme Court. Knight argued Alabama's case. In *Powell v. Alabama*, the ILD lawyers wanted to prove the Scottsboro Boys were not given fair access to choose their own counsel. This was a violation of the Fourteenth Amendment to the Constitution. They also reasserted that the trials should have been moved because the environment of the trials could have influenced jurors. The fact that it stayed in Scottsboro, the lawyers said, was in violation of the Sixth Amendment.

THE DECISION

The US Supreme Court overturned the Alabama Supreme Court decision on November 7, writing that to execute the prisoners without a retrial would be "judicial murder."[2] Justice George Sutherland of the Supreme Court found that the appointment of the defense was done in an informal way. He explained:

> *During perhaps the most critical periods of the proceedings against these defendants, that is to say, from the time of their arraignment until the beginning of their trial, when*

consultation, thorough-going investigation, and preparation were vitally important, the defendants did not have the aid of counsel in any real sense, although they were as much entitled to such aid during that period as at the trial itself.[3]

The court noted that the accused did not have sufficient counsel and that their lawyers had been essentially forced upon them, ruling that the Fourteenth Amendment had been violated. The court ruled that the defendants had been deprived of due process of the law and denied equal protection of the law.

As for the argument that the Sixth Amendment was violated, the court upheld the Alabama Supreme Court decision. The court felt there was no evidence the juries' decisions were influenced by the presence of the National Guard, the number of people in Scottsboro, or the celebration after the Weems and Norris decision. The court said it would not impose upon the rights of a state to set up its own guidelines for how and when a jury could be chosen. The ILD lawyers made it clear they would put this decision to the test in the next trials.

Shower stalls in Kilby Prison

At Kilby Prison

Meanwhile, the young men stayed at Kilby Prison on death row. Norris remembered the routine there:

> *At Kilby, we were caged in narrow cells with small windows which prevented you from seeing anything except a few cells directly in front of you and the guards when they came by. . . .*

Executed in Their Stead

Although the execution dates for the boys had been put off, the boys were still housed in death row of Kilby Prison. On July 10, 1931, the original date set for their electrocution, another prisoner, Will Stokes, was executed. Patterson recalled, "If I live to be a hundred I will never forget that day. . . . When they turned on the juice for Stokes we could hear the z-z-z-z-z-z of the electric current outside in the death row. The buzz went several times. After the juice was squeezed into him a guard came out and gave us a report. 'Stokes died hard. They stuck a needle through his head to make sure.' I sweated my clothes wet."[5]

You could talk with prisoners on either side of you, but you were never allowed outside your cell unless all the other prisoners were locked in their cells. When you were allowed to take a shower, there would be two guards standing there as you left your cell, naked. . . . They would march you to the bathroom for a 3- or 4-minute shower.[4]

The Scottsboro Boys and their supporters were about to get another chance to prove their innocence to an audience that wanted them to be guilty. But, first, they needed a top-notch attorney.

Prisoners were put to work sewing in the clothing department at Kilby Prison.

Some of the Scottsboro Boys were escorted to the Decatur courtroom under heavy armed guard.

THE RETRIAL

After the Supreme Court ruling, the ILD decided the case was so high profile they needed a high-profile trial lawyer. In January 1933, they chose Samuel Leibowitz, an accomplished lawyer from New York City. The ILD admitted they were unable to pay Leibowitz for working on the case, but Leibowitz agreed to take it on anyway. While Leibowitz was not interested in the Communist cause, he was interested in the worldwide notoriety the case was gaining. Leibowitz did not realize the tactics and methods that won him fame in New York would become one of his greatest challenges in Alabama.

The Supreme Court ordered the trial be moved. But instead of moving the trial to the much larger city of Montgomery, the new trial would be held in Decatur, Alabama, a town not far from and not much bigger than Scottsboro.

Leibowitz was successful in getting the young men tried separately. The first to be tried, Leibowitz decided, would be Patterson. Leibowitz chose Patterson because he best fit the southern stereotype of a black rapist. He was surly and sullen, hardened by years of getting by on his own from an early age.

The prosecutor would once again be Alabama Attorney General Thomas Knight. He shared a common trait with his adversary Leibowitz: ambition.

The judge for the trial was James Horton, who was known for his integrity and respected by the community. Horton was described as being Abraham Lincoln-esque, having a similar bearing, look, and sense of justice as the former president.

Jury selections were made, and again the jury was all male and all white. During the pretrial, Leibowitz attempted to draw out the racism of the process by which the jury was selected. He presented many black professionals that somehow did not fit the requirements to be selected. Though Leibowitz felt he had exposed the prejudice of the jury system in the Decatur court, Judge Horton became exasperated and ended the discussion.

Leibowitz and Jury Selection

Leibowitz tried to get the case thrown out because the jury selection had been prejudicial. To make his point he called to the stand those on the jury commission who were responsible for jury selection. One of these men was Stockton Benson, editor of a local paper, the *Scottsboro Progressive Age*. Benson said that African Americans lacked good judgment and were therefore not even considered in the process. When Leibowitz asked if the black reverends and teachers had good judgment, Benson responded that "some of them has got education enough . . . but, as a matter of a fact, I think they wouldn't have the character . . . Yes Sir. They will nearly all steal."[1]

Leibowitz then called the head of the jury commission, J. E. Moody, who also asserted that blacks were not intentionally excluded from the jury rolls. Leibowitz asked the legal requirements of a juror, to which Moody responded that he could only remember that a juror was to have character. Moody explained to Leibowitz that there was no conspiracy to exclude blacks, they were never even considered part of the equation. They were, in fact, not mentioned at all.

THE PATTERSON TRIAL BEGINS

The trial of Patterson began on March 27, 1933. Knight called his first witness, Price, who repeated the same tale she had told four times before. She again explained why she and Bates were on the train, that they had been looking for work in Chattanooga and were returning to their homes in Montgomery. She told about the fight between the black and white boys on the train and her subsequent rape. She identified Patterson as one of the rapists.

When the cross-examination began, Price faced an attorney for the first time who did not assume her story was true. A battle began between Price and Leibowitz. At the beginning of the cross-examination, Leibowitz produced a toy train, an exact replica, representing the train where the alleged crime took place. When asked, Price would admit in no way the similarity between the toy and

The Southern Perception of Leibowitz

The difference between northern and southern perceptions of Leibowitz and his handling of the trial was great. While praised for his prowess in the courtroom by the northern press, the southern press had quite a different take. The southern *Sylacauga News* reported, "One possessed of that old southern chivalry cannot read the trial now in progress in Decatur . . . and publish an opinion and keep within the law. [Leibowitz's] brutal manner . . . makes one feel like reaching for his gun while his blood boils to the nth degree."[2]

Leibowitz used a model of the freight train to expose contradictions in the witnesses' testimonies.

the real train. Leibowitz asked in what way was the train different, to which she snapped, "That is not the train I was on. It was bigger, lots bigger, that is a toy."[3] To any other questions about the differences between the trains, Price refused to answer.

Leibowitz continued his cross-examination. At one point, he asked about Callie Brochie's boardinghouse, where Price and Bates allegedly stayed during their night in Chattanooga. Price recalled specific details about Brochie and her house, including its address. Leibowitz revealed that a search of all of Chattanooga had been done, and no Callie Brochie had been found. Leibowitz asked Price if she made up Brochie, using the name of the character, Callie Brochie, published in stories in a popular magazine. Price denied this.

Leibowitz called a young drifter, Lester Carter, to the witness stand. Carter said that a few days before the alleged rapes, he and a friend had met Price and Bates and went for an evening walk. After passing a hobo camp, they made a fire, and Carter began to have sexual intercourse with Bates. He looked over and saw his

Southern Womanhood

Leibowitz's treatment of Price on the witness stand deeply offended many southerners. An observer commented that "Leibowitz made the fatal mistake of regarding Price as a cut-rate prostitute. He was 'not accustomed to addressing Southern juries'. . . . Too late the chief defense attorney realized that Mrs. Price had become a symbol of white Southern womanhood."[4]

Early in the trial, a group of 200 men, angered by Leibowitz's handling of Price on the stand, met in a hall near the courthouse to openly protest Leibowitz's cross-examination of Price. The group openly discussed taking matters into their own hands, running Leibowitz out of town on a rail and lynching the defendants.

Patterson took the witness stand in his own defense on April 7, 1933.

friend having sexual intercourse with Price. When asked, Price said she had no knowledge of Carter at all.

At the end of the first day of the trial, northern papers sang Leibowitz's praises for the precision of his cross-examination. The southern papers had a different take: Leibowitz's cross-examination of Price was an affront to southern womanhood and the south itself.

A Surprise Witness

On April 6, the Patterson trial continued on. In a surprise move, Leibowitz called Ruby Bates to the stand. She had been thought to be in hiding, but the CPUSA had tracked her down in New York. She sat on the stand in a new dress, answering Leibowitz's questions. Yes, she said, she had seen Price having sexual intercourse the night before the incident. She also admitted that she had only followed along with Price's story about the rape to avoid serving time for hoboing.

If Bates was the defense's dynamite, Knight was about to snip the fuse. When Knight cross-examined her, he asked her where she got her clothes and who had been paying her bills. Her answer was that the Communists had paid for everything. From that moment on, Bates was discredited in the eyes of the jury.

Too late would Leibowitz realize that his lack of understanding of southern culture would play heavily in his defense. The Scottsboro Boys were not the only ones on trial in Decatur: so was Leibowitz. To southerners he symbolized the essence of the northern invader, someone who had moved from the north to the disadvantaged south to profit after the Civil War. Leibowitz was Jewish and now had an affiliation with Communists—both groups many southerners distrusted. Knight, in his closing arguments, cried, "Show them that Alabama justice cannot be bought and sold with Jew money from New York."[5]

When the trial ended on April 9, the jury returned with a guilty verdict. For the second time, Haywood Patterson was sentenced to death. ⌐

"In the face of the feeling which exists at Decatur as well as throughout the Tennessee Valley against any lawyer claiming to represent the International Labor Defense, we suggest that it would not be well for these lawyers to show up on any soil at any point within the valley. We do not need that type of cattle down here and their further appearance is wholly unnecessary."[6]

—*Huntsville Community Builder*

Ruby Bates during the retrial of Haywood Patterson in Decatur, Alabama

Leibowitz's status as a northerner may have hurt Patterson at his retrial in Decatur.

TRIED AGAIN

Leibowitz was stunned by the guilty verdict in Decatur. He now realized that he was on trial as well as the young men. Upon his return to New York, however, he was hailed as a hero. As he departed the train, he was hoisted upon the shoulders of crowd members as cheers rang out. He bitterly lamented to the papers the primitive state of the south and southerners in general. He spoke at rallies in support of the movement to free the young men.

Meanwhile, the cause of the Scottsboro Boys was discussed and demonstrated around the world. Blacks and whites were protesting together. This represented a significant aspect of the movement to free the Scottsboro Boys. Whites and blacks were marching and working together toward a common goal. Not since the abolitionist movement had blacks and whites worked together in such a way for social justice. This joining of forces set the scene for the powerful civil rights movement of the 1950s and 1960s.

HORTON'S DOUBTS

Judge Horton convened court to hear motions for a new trial from

Leibowitz Shares His Views

Returning to New York, Leibowitz lost his composure and strongly criticized the jurors and, in effect, all of the south. "If you ever saw those creatures, those bigots whose mouths are slits in their faces, whose eyes pop out like a frog's, whose chins drip tobacco juice, bewhiskered and filthy, you would not ask how they could do it."[1] Leibowitz said that after the two-week trial in Decatur, he needed a "moral, mental, and physical bath."[2]

the defense. He himself had been moved to question the truthfulness of the testimony in the case. He wondered why were there no cuts on Price's head when the doctors examined her if a blow with a pistol butt had truly cut Price's head, as she had testified. He also called into question the amount of sperm in the girls' bodies. He could not see how six men would leave so little sperm, and the sperm being nonmotile gave him doubts as well. He commented,

> *The conclusion becomes clear and clearer that this woman was not forced into intercourse with all of these negroes upon that train, but that her condition was clearly due to the intercourse she had had on the nights previous to this time.*[3]

On June 22, Horton declared that he was setting aside the verdict and sentence for the Patterson trial. Patterson would be tried again. Initially, after the trial in Decatur, Horton had been hailed. Now, he faced disgrace. He was encouraged to withdraw from the next Scottsboro trials.

Judge William Callahan

On October 20, Judge William Callahan was selected by the state to try the case instead of Horton. Where Horton was studied and deliberative,

Demonstrators led a hooded figure representing Judge Callahan in a protest marking the third anniversary of the Scottsboro Boys' arrests.

Callahan was not. Callahan, as the *New York Herald Tribune* put it, got his education not in college, but after reading books in his father's barn. Callahan, at age 70, sat for the bar at an earlier time when lawyers did not have to have a degree. Unlike Horton, Callahan provided no press passes for African-American reporters. He kept a rule of strict silence in the court and allowed no pictures. He was all business and did not allow anything he saw as extraneous to getting the young men tried and convicted. His aim was finishing the trial he felt had "become involved in a tangle of extraneous matters relative to Communist activities among the Negroes, interference of outsiders with Alabama justice and local pride."[4]

There had been the threat of mob violence in the previous trial, which Horton had curtailed with the active presence of the National Guard. Since the retrial at Decatur was set, there was a rash of lynching across the United States, particularly in the south. Just before the trial was to start, two ILD lawyers had been shot to death while representing black defendants in another part of Alabama. Leibowitz argued that the Guard should be sent in to maintain peace during the proceedings. Callahan flatly denied the request. Eventually, Callahan assigned two

Violence during the Trial

The threat of violence was greater than ever as the second trial got underway. In Alabama and in other states, lynching became more common. In Tuscaloosa, Alabama, three African-American men were lynched after being charged with rape and murder. There was more lynching in Louisiana and Maryland. The atmosphere was so volatile that the Alabama governor sent 15 men to guard the Scottsboro Boys' defense team.

The defense team, from left: *Samuel Leibowitz, George Chamlee, and Joseph Brodsky*

guards to protect Leibowitz and the concerned Alabama governor sent 15 deputies. Leibowitz himself brought in two New York City homicide detectives as bodyguards.

More Trials

The retrial of Patterson began on November 20, 1933. Callahan, concerned about the increasing expense of the trials, announced that the trial would be finished in three days, although ultimately the trial would take more than a week. Patterson's trial had taken approximately two weeks in Judge Horton's court. Leibowitz requested that the trial be moved and was denied. He then asked that the previous indictments of the young men be thrown out due to the fact that there were no African Americans on the jury. Callahan also denied that request.

Leibowitz not only had to face Knight again, but now he had to contend with the prejudiced Callahan as well. When Price began contradicting herself on the stand, Callahan cut Leibowitz short, urging him to move on to something important. Crucial evidence was disallowed. Callahan openly mocked Leibowitz and at times commanded him to sit down.

Race and the Jury

J. A. Tidwell, a member of the Morgan County Jury Commission, was responsible for putting potential jurors' names on the jury rolls. He explained that he did not consider race when naming potential jurors, but he did consider other factors. His explanation reveals the racist stereotypes that many people held about African Americans:

I do not know of any negro in Morgan County over 21 and under 65 who is generally reputed to be honest and intelligent and who is esteemed in the community for his integrity, good character and sound judgment, who is not an habitual drunkard, who isn't afflicted with a permanent disease or physical weakness which would render him unfit to discharge the duties of a juror, who can read English, and who has never been convicted of a crime involving moral [wickedness].[5]

The trial moved toward its conclusion. On the final day of the trial, November 30, Knight appealed to the passions of the men in the courtroom to protect the womanhood of Alabama. Callahan himself took up the white cause in his instructions to the jury. He informed them that in any rape case where the woman is white and the man is black, the jury should presume the guilt of the defendant. And that if the defendant, Patterson in this case, was at the scene of the crime for:

> aiding, encouraging, assisting or abetting in any way the commission of the crime [he should be considered] as guilty as the one who committed the offense, although he never moved a muscle or said a word.[6]

Callahan instructed the jury as to the forms their verdict could take: from the most severe, the death penalty, to a prison term no less than ten years. But he added that the term could be as long as the jury felt applicable. As the jury prepared to leave the room, Leibowitz quickly approached the bench followed by Knight. Callahan neglected to mention that there was another sentencing option. A quick, whispered conference ensued, then Callahan addressed the jurors. "I believe I forgot one thing about the forms of the verdict," he said.[7] Then, he instructed the jury about the requirements for returning a not guilty verdict.

After a brief deliberation, the jury decided Patterson's fate. Judge Callahan announced to the court that Patterson had been found guilty of rape and that his sentence was death.

Norris's case followed with jury selection the next afternoon, December 1. It proceeded much like Patterson's case. And it was no surprise when the jury returned a guilty verdict and a death sentence on December 5. After reading the decision for Norris, Callahan neglected to invoke the mercy of God, which was traditionally done when the death sentence was given.

Leibowitz asked that the remaining trials be postponed, and Callahan agreed. Leibowitz returned to New York, dumbfounded and dejected. ⌐

The jury for the retrial of Haywood Patterson

Four of the Scottsboro Boys, Eugene Williams, Olin Montgomery, Willie Roberson, and Roy Wright, with their attorney, Samuel Leibowitz

SUPREME COURT JUSTICE

Though suffering the defeats in the Alabama courts, Leibowitz was undeterred. In June 1934, he appealed the Patterson and Norris guilty verdicts to the Alabama Supreme Court on the grounds that there were no African Americans on the jury rolls and that Callahan had prejudiced the jury by neglecting to instruct them about a not-guilty verdict.

Knight again represented the state of Alabama. He asked that the appeal be thrown out, due to the defense not submitting the paperwork for an appeal in time. And it was true. The defense team had submitted the paperwork late, but they had done so only because Callahan misinformed them about the process. Knight also argued that it was not the state's right to decide who would be on the jury roll. He said it was the duty of the local jury commission to select potential jurors.

The court listened to Knight's arguments. On June 28, the court denied Leibowitz's request for a new trial on the basis that the defense was late in submitting the proper papers. In addition, the court found there was no discrimination evident

Jury Risks

Alabama State Senator J. Miller Bonner sponsored a bill to keep blacks off juries by excluding those who were not eligible to vote. Others commented that this was too much trouble. They thought that any blacks on the jury rolls could be eliminated once jury selection started. The assumption was that no African American would want to risk serving on a jury in Alabama and that they would all ask to be excused.

in the jury rolls. The court said the rolls reflected those potential jurors that met the requirements. Patterson was sentenced to die on August 31, 1934. Leibowitz and the ILD legal team now hoped to appeal the case to the US Supreme Court, but there would be complications.

GETTING TO THE US SUPREME COURT

One such complication involved getting the case tried at all. Since the defense missed the paperwork deadline in the Patterson case, the case was never considered officially appealed to the Alabama Supreme Court. The US Supreme Court could not hear a case that had not been tried by a state supreme court. Patterson's case was in a sort of limbo. The defense filed for a rehearing of the Patterson case in the Alabama Supreme Court. His execution date was postponed.

Another complication arose on October 1, 1934, when police arrested two ILD lawyers in Nashville, Tennessee, for attempting to bribe Price into changing her testimony. The ILD lawyers and another man, acting as a go-between, were arrested for offering Price $500, and later an additional $1,000, to recant her rape claims. Price had contacted the police, who encouraged her to go along with the plan.

Leibowitz was angry when he found out about the plan and the arrests. He publicly denied any knowledge of the bribery attempt and issued a statement saying as much. He wrote that he could not "continue as counsel in the Scottsboro case until the Communists are removed," cutting all ties with the ILD and the CPUSA.[1] He went on to imply that the Communists had raised a large amount of money from the Scottsboro case,

Leibowitz Responds

After two ILD lawyers were caught trying to bribe Price, Leibowitz issued a statement:

I knew nothing of the activities of the two men from the International Labor Defense who were arrested in Nashville, charged with attempting to bribe Victoria Price. The defense needed no such help. . . . Until all secret maneuverings, ballyhoo, mass pressure and Communist methods are removed from the case, I can no longer continue. I am not deserting the Scottsboro boys. I have given of my best and am prepared to continue to do so to the end that the Scottsboro boys shall not die.[2]

The ILD responded in kind. In the *Daily Worker*, the CPUSA's paper, Leibowitz's response was deemed an act of treachery and slander. The *Daily Worker* went on to say that the only reason Leibowitz was withdrawing from the case was due to Patterson and Norris signing with Wallace Pollak, the lawyer who had previously represented them successfully in front of the Supreme Court. Meanwhile, Leibowitz helped organize the American Scottsboro Committee so he could continue the defense of the young men.

Leibowitz conferred with seven of the defendants on May 1, 1935.
Left to right: *Deputy Sheriff Charles McComb, Leibowitz, Roy Wright, Montgomery, Powell, Roberson, Williams, Weems, and Andy Wright.*

yet he provided his services for free. The ILD fired back, issuing a statement saying that Leibowitz had put himself and his ambition before anything else.

In the meantime, the Alabama Supreme Court declined to rehear the appeal. However, the defense asked the US Supreme Court to review the legality of the Decatur trial itself. Using a legal action known as a writ of certiorari, the US Supreme Court agreed to examine the constitutionality of the trial.

Choosing the Defense

A dispute began over who would defend Patterson and Norris before the Supreme Court. A group of ministers from Harlem convinced both Patterson and Norris to sign with Leibowitz. Shortly thereafter, the two men signed affidavits saying they wanted the ILD to represent them, then signed with Leibowitz again.

In the meantime, Leibowitz went to the NAACP for help. But as before, the NAACP did not want to be associated with the Communists in any way. Leibowitz was, however, able to garner support from a group of African Americans in Harlem. They formed the American Scottsboro Committee (ASC). The chairman was Dr. George E. Haynes from the Federal Council of Churches and the director was the editor from a black newspaper, the *Amsterdam News*. With the backing of the ASC,

Racist Jury Selection

The Supreme Court found that the selection process for the jury was prejudicial and that Leibowitz's objections to the jury selection process should have been upheld in Callahan's court. One Supreme Court justice commented that it was impossible to accept that all of the African Americans in Morgan County were unqualified to serve on a jury. He went on to say that, according to the evidence, there were so many qualified African Americans that it invalidated the jury commissioner's testimony.

Changes for Jury Selection in Alabama

After the Supreme Court reversed the Norris and Patterson verdicts, Alabama Governor David Bibb Graves sent a notice to all the solicitors and judges in Alabama. He wrote, "Whether Alabamians like it or not, it is the patriotic duty of every citizen and the sworn duty of every public officer to accept and uphold them in letter and in spirit. The action of the nation's highest court means that we must put the names of Negroes in jury boxes in every county."[3]

Leibowitz would represent Patterson and Norris. Before the trial began on February 15, 1935, Patterson had jumped ship again. He decided to let the ILD represent him for the Supreme Court case.

In Norris's case before the Supreme Court, *Norris v. Alabama*, Leibowitz brought the jury rolls of the second Decatur trials for the justices to examine. The justices examined the rolls and found there were names of African Americans on the rolls. The issue was that these names had obviously been added at a later date. The names were scrawled in between lines and at the bottom of pages. The Supreme Court found the forgery of the names reprehensible. But what was worse, they found, was the blatant history of discrimination against qualified African Americans and their right to stand on a jury. The court overturned Norris's conviction on April 1.

Leibowitz had won Norris a new trial. The court, seeing the similarities between the Norris and Patterson cases, granted Patterson a retrial as well.

Handwriting expert J. Vreeland Haring testified that the names of black men had been illegally submitted to the previously all-white grand jury rolls.

After being held at a jail in Birmingham, Alabama, seven of the Scottsboro defendants were escorted into the courthouse in Decatur.

BACK TO ALABAMA

The Scottsboro Boys faced a round of new trials, again with the contentious Judge Callahan presiding. Leibowitz would be representing eight of the nine young men. Patterson was the only one to refuse Leibowitz. Patterson asked to be represented by the ILD. The ILD, however, was facing even more hurdles in the south now. Not only were they seen as being Communists and northern outsiders, but with their links to the attempt to bribe Price, they were seen as illegally influencing the trial. In 1935, representatives of the ILD, NAACP, ASC, and the American Civil Liberties Union (ACLU), groups that had openly criticized one another, formed the Scottsboro Defense Committee (SDC) and began working together. Allan Knight Chalmers was chairman and served as a defense attorney.

The committee felt Leibowitz had become a liability. It decided Leibowitz would still remain as counsel for the defense, but in a supporting capacity. The SDC decided to hire a southern lawyer. They decided upon Clarence L. Watts, who was hired at a steep price. Watts was a Huntsville, Alabama, native.

The Trials Begin

The trials began on January 20, 1936, with little fanfare. The Scottsboro Boys waited their turns in the Birmingham Jail. The crowds that swarmed the first trials were gone. Alabamians were growing weary of the trial. While many were still raging against what many felt was an insult to the womanhood of Alabama, there were some Alabama residents who were now concerned about the drain the trials had become on the state's funds and the bad press Alabama was receiving.

Patterson's trial was first. It was very similar to the previous trials. Even though 12 African-American men were in the jury pool, 12 white men were selected to sit on the jury. Price gave her familiar testimony, and so did the defendants. In his closing arguments for the prosecution, Melvin Hutson entreated the jury, yelling that they needed to put aside the evidence and quickly return a guilty verdict.

And they did. After approximately eight hours of deliberation, the jury announced it had reached a

---

Different Opinions

The southern and northern press interpreted Patterson's 75-year sentence differently. The southern response was outrage. The *Birmingham Age Herald* reported that the Patterson sentence "represents probably the first time in the history of the South that a Negro has been convicted of a charge of rape upon a white woman and has been given less than a death sentence."[1] The *New York Times*, on the other hand, was more optimistic about the verdict:

As three previous juries had voted for a death sentence, this is a sign that the temper of Alabama juries has at least slightly changed. Whether because of the manner in which the defense was this time conducted, or because the years of outside criticism and the attitude of the Supreme Court have at last begun to take effect, the Scottsboro boys can now regard their case as not altogether hopeless.[2]

verdict on January 23. Again, Patterson was found guilty as charged. But this time when the sentence was announced, something different happened. No death sentence was handed down. All present were shocked. An African American had been found guilty of raping a white woman in the state of Alabama and had not been sentenced to death. One juror, having deep suspicion that Price had lied on the witness stand, held out against the death penalty. In a deal with the other jurors, Patterson's sentence was not to be death in the electric chair, but 75 years in prison.

The Ride Back to Prison

On January 24, the boys were loaded three to a police car and transported back to the Birmingham Jail. In the rear seat of one of the squad cars, Roy Wright sat on the left handcuffed to Norris in the middle, and Powell sat on the right cuffed to Norris. There are varying reports of what exactly happened, but during the ride to the jail, there was an exchange between Powell and the

A "Remarkable" Compromise

A reporter for northern newspaper the *New Republic* commented that it would be hard for those from the north to think the 75-year sentence represented anything other than a defeat. "But," the reporter continued, "when one realizes that the state in its plea never suggested an alternative for the death penalty . . . and that the Judge broadly hinted as to the necessity of the extreme penalty, the compromise becomes all the more remarkable."[3]

Weems was escorted back to prison after being sentenced to 75 years.

officer in the front passenger seat. The exchange
turned violent when Powell pulled out a concealed
knife and slashed the officer's throat. The officer
driving slammed on the brakes, pulling the police
car to the side of the road. The bleeding officer fled
the car, while the driver pulled his gun and fired
into the back seat, striking Powell in the head. The
wounded officer was rushed to the nearest hospital,

as was Powell. Both survived, though Powell suffered brain damage.

The Rest of the Trials

After some political wrangling, trying to make a deal to finally conclude the case of the Scottsboro Boys, the discussion fell apart. The same cast of characters appeared in Judge Callahan's court yet again. The exception was that Thomas Knight, who had long served on the prosecution team, died in May 1937, shortly before the trials were to resume.

Norris's trial took place from July 12 to July 16, 1937. He was found guilty again and sentenced to death. Head defense attorney Watts fell ill, so Leibowitz took over the defense again. Andy Wright's trial followed from July 20 to July 21. As in the Patterson decision, Wright was not sentenced to death. His sentence was 99 years in prison.

Weems's trial followed from July 22 to July 23. Weems was found guilty, but instead of the 1,000-year sentence the prosecutor suggested,

The Stabbing

Predictably, there were different versions of the stabbing in the police car. Sheriff Sandlin, who was driving the squad car, stated that while Powell was attacking Deputy Blalock, Roy Wright pulled a knife and attacked Sandlin with his free left hand. Roy Wright denied the Sheriff's claim, saying, "I didn't have a knife, and I didn't try to cut the sheriff. I know he would have killed me. . . . We wouldn't try to escape now that things look better for all of us."[4]

the jury gave Weems 75 years in prison. Powell's trial was next, from July 23 to July 24. He was being tried for knifing the officer on the way to the Birmingham Jail. Powell pleaded guilty as charged and received the maximum sentence of 20 years behind bars.

A Surprise

After Powell's sentence on July 24, something Leibowitz described as miraculous happened. The state's attorney, Thomas Lawson, approached the bench and informed Judge Callahan that the state was dropping the charges against the four remaining defendants. Olen Montgomery, Willie Roberson, Eugene Williams, and Roy Wright were free.

Leibowitz hurried across the street to the jail, presented the release order, and whisked the four confused boys into waiting cars. The cars carrying the boys were given a police escort to the Alabama state line. Four of the Scottsboro nine were free. There would be no more Scottsboro trials. ⌐

Price Responds to the Patterson Verdict

Many southerners felt that less than the death penalty for Patterson was an injustice. Price was among them. After the jury returned the 75-year sentence, Price commented that she did not think it was enough. Years later, after the boys were released, Price would continue to repeat the rape story.

*A crowd at Penn Station greeted Montgomery, center, and Williams, right,
in New York on July 26, 1937.*

Samuel Leibowitz, center, and four of the freed Scottsboro Boys celebrate their release in New York City.

THE BITTER END

Though there would be no more Scottsboro Boys' trials in Alabama, the fate of the five young men who remained in jail still hung in the balance. They would face years of unsuccessful parole hearings.

Patterson's appeal to the Supreme Court after his sentence was unsuccessful. His 75-year sentence would stand. This decision gave the other boys' attorneys little hope of appealing the verdicts for them. After this defeat, attorney Chalmers, who was representing the young men who remained in prison, attempted to work out a deal with Alabama Governor Graves. Even though Graves privately supported the release of the remaining boys, he refused to put anything on paper that would bind him. When Chalmers tried to apply pressure, Graves implored him to have patience. Graves finally commuted Norris's sentence to life in prison, as opposed to the original death sentence, in July 1938.

LIVING WITH FREEDOM

Meanwhile on the outside, the four young men who had been released faced new challenges. They had been released so suddenly that Leibowitz and other supporters were caught off guard with no plan for how to deal with them. It was Leibowitz's intention to start the young men at vocational schools. Leibowitz explained this was his attempt to "resurrect lives almost crushed out of them by the relentless persecution of the state of Alabama."[1]

Even though Leibowitz forbade any exploitation of the young men, they were swarmed with offers as soon as they set foot in New York. A black minister from Brooklyn, who was known for his moneymaking schemes, convinced them to sign with him as their manager. He promised them a life in show business. He convinced them Leibowitz was using them to make money. As a result, the four broke all ties with Leibowitz.

The first performance of the former defendants was at Harlem's famous Apollo Theater, where they were billed as "the symbol of a struggle for enlightenment and human brotherhood which will go on and on until it is won!"[2]

Antilynching Bill

In the mid-1930s, opponents of lynching had won the support of Senators Robert F. Wagner and Edward Costigan. Wagner and Costigan drafted an antilynching bill that made law enforcement officers responsible for the safety of persons in their custody. Officers who neglected this duty would be punishable in federal court. However, the bill was met with opposition. Even though First Lady Eleanor Roosevelt was a supporter, her husband, President Franklin D. Roosevelt refused to support the legislation. He feared if he supported the bill he would lose support from white southerners and therefore the presidential election.

In the meantime, lynching still continued. A white woman swore a complaint against Rubin Stacy, an African American, and while he was being transported by six deputies, a lynch mob seized Stacy. They dragged him to the house of the woman who made the complaint and hung him from a tree. Later, it was found that Stacy had done no harm to the woman but had only surprised her when he came begging by her back door for food. Even the case of Stacy did not sway Roosevelt.

To their disappointment, the four found that show business was run much like sharecropping. Their manager took a large percentage of their profits. The Apollo made them buy new suits and accessories. By the end of the week, not only had they spent the advance given to them, but they actually owed money. They broke ties with their manager and went back to the SDC for help. After that, many of the young men split up to make their own ways in the world.

Montgomery took music lessons, playing the guitar and saxophone. However, he struggled with money and drinking and never made it as a musician. Williams moved to Saint Louis, Missouri, to be with his family. Roy attended a vocational school, joined the army, and married. However, in 1959, Roy killed his wife after finding her at another man's home. Roy then returned to his own apartment and

Harsh Imprisonment

The stress of day-to-day imprisonment wore on the young men. Before his release, Montgomery explained in a letter home, "You always want to know how I am getting along. You ought to know just how I feel with out asking. If you stay in Jail six years how would you feel. You wouldn't even want no one to ask you that. In other words you people up there will help run a person insane the way you all act. I writes you and ask you to do things and you wont even answer. But yet you always wants to know how some Body is feeling and getting along. How can I feel up lifted?"[3]

shot himself. Roberson suffered from asthma. In jail, he had complained that there were times when he could hardly breathe. Roberson was charged with disorderly conduct after a fight broke out in a bar where he was. He swore his innocence. Roberson eventually died from an asthma attack.

THE OTHER FIVE

Back in Alabama, Governor Graves went back on his promise to release the five Scottsboro Boys who were still in prison, Norris, Powell Patterson, Weems, and Andy Wright. He had interviewed each in his office and found them illiterate and contemptible. Chalmers suspected Graves had pulled out of the deal due to political pressure, and Graves admitted as much in a conversation with Chalmers.

Tuskegee Institute doctor G. C. Branche visited the five in prison in January 1937. At that point they had been in solitary confinement for a year. He interviewed and examined

"I just think about getting out of here. That's all I want to do. That's the only thing that will bring happiness to me. I'm just being held here because I'm [black]. That's why I'm in jail; not nothing I've done."[4]

—Olen Montgomery

Patterson served 12 years of his 75-year prison term before escaping.

the young men. He found Patterson to be angry and suspicious. Patterson felt used by the Communists and used by Leibowitz to make money and gain publicity. Powell, who had been shot in the head, had trouble remembering things and was weak on one side of his body.

After the release of four of the Scottsboro Boys, the SDC and Norris assumed the governor was going to commute the other boys' sentences. When this did not happen, Norris, the only one with a death sentence, began to suspect that he was used as a bargaining chip in a deal to let the others go free. In a letter, he wrote, "I say you all framed me to the Electric Chair and the others in prison with a lifetime for the freedom of the other four boys. . . . I just soon to be Dead than to be treated like I have been Treated by you all. I Believe all of you all just as much against me as that old lying woman that caused me to suffer near Seven Years."[5]

Freedom for the young men would be a long time coming. In November 1943, Weems and Andy Wright were paroled. Weems took a job at a laundry in Atlanta, Georgia, married, and stayed out of the public eye. Andy had a job in Montgomery, but later escaped to the north, violating his parole. The SDC convinced Andy to return, and Andy was again imprisoned. In 1944, Andy and Norris were released, but were returned to jail after violating their parole. Powell and Norris were paroled in the summer and fall of 1946 respectively, 15 years after their arrest. Powell moved to Georgia, while Norris again violated his parole. He pretended to be his brother and found work. Norris was arrested under his brother's name three times, for having a gun, for gambling, and for stabbing his girlfriend.

Norris was finally released from Kilby Prison in 1946.

In July 1948 while on a work detail, Patterson escaped. He headed north, never to set foot in the south again. Andy was paroled for a third time in June 1950, and the same month, Federal Bureau of

> "This place is killing me, I don't see why we innocent boys should be kept here all this time for nothing."[7]
>
> —Patterson, after a year in solitary confinement

Investigation (FBI) agents captured Patterson in Michigan. Patterson was not sent back to Alabama, however, because the governor of Michigan refused to sign his extradition papers. Later that year, Patterson was charged with murder. He died of cancer in prison in 1952.

Meanwhile, Andy's former girlfriend accused him of raping her foster daughter in 1951. Andy spent another eight months in jail before being proven innocent of the crime. After that, Andy had a difficult time finding work. He settled in Albany, New York, but when he stabbed his wife in a fight, he was forced to leave the state.

In October 1976, 45 years after the Scottsboro Boys were arrested in Paint Rock, Alabama, avowed segregationist Alabama Governor George Wallace pardoned Norris, who was married with children and the last living Scottsboro Boy. Norris traveled to Alabama to personally receive his pardon. Norris stated that he had no ill feelings toward the ones who persecuted him. "I only wish," said Norris, "the other eight boys could be here today—their lives were ruined by this thing too."[6]

Governor George Wallace of Alabama was known for his support
of racial segregation early in his political career.

TIMELINE

1931	1931	1932
On March 25, nine African-American youths are pulled from a train in Paint Rock, Alabama, and accused of raping two white women.	The first trial is held from April 6 to April 9. Eight young men are found guilty and sentenced to death. Roy Wright's trial ends in a mistrial.	The ILD appeals the verdicts to the Supreme Court of Alabama. Court proceedings begin on January 21.

1933	1933	1933
On April 9, Patterson is found guilty and is again sentenced to death.	Judge Horton reviews the Patterson decision and overturns the verdict and the sentence on June 22. Horton grants a new trial.	Patterson and Clarence Norris are tried again in November and early December. Both are sentenced to death.

1932	**1932**	**1933**
On March 25, the court upholds the death sentences for seven of the eight young men.	*Powell v. Alabama* is appealed to the US Supreme Court. The verdict is overturned on November 7.	Haywood Patterson is tried again on March 27 in Decatur, Alabama. Judge James Horton presides. The defense lawyer is Samuel Leibowitz.

1934	**1934**	**1935**
The Alabama Supreme Court upholds the convictions of Patterson and Norris on June 28.	On October 1, two ILD lawyers are arrested for trying to bribe Victoria Price into changing her testimony.	The US Supreme Court hears *Norris v. Alabama* on February 15. Leibowitz is the attorney for the defense.

TIMELINE

1935

On April 1, the US Supreme Court overturns the Norris verdict.

1936

Patterson stands trial again. He is found guilty on January 23 and receives a 75-year sentence.

1936

On January 24, while being transported, Ozie Powell slashes the throat of a deputy sheriff. Powell is shot in the head. Both men recover.

1937

From July 23 to July 24, Powell pleads guilty to stabbing an officer and is given a sentence of 20 years.

1937

On July 24, all charges against Olen Montgomery, Willie Roberson, Eugene Williams, and Roy Wright are dropped.

1937	1937	1937
From July 12 to July 16, Norris is tried in Judge William Callahan's court. He is found guilty and sentenced to death.	From July 20 to July 21, Andy Wright is tried, found guilty, and sentenced to 99 years in prison.	From July 22 to July 23, Charles Weems is tried, convicted, and given a sentence of 75 years.

1938	1976
In July, Governor David Graves reduces Norris's death sentence to life in prison.	Alabama governor and avowed segregationist George Wallace pardons Norris in October.

ESSENTIAL FACTS

DATE OF EVENT

March 25, 1931 to October 1976

PLACE OF EVENT

- ❖ Scottsboro, Alabama
- ❖ Paint Rock, Alabama
- ❖ Decatur, Alabama

KEY PLAYERS

- ❖ Ruby Bates
- ❖ Samuel Leibowitz
- ❖ Olen Montgomery
- ❖ Clarence Norris
- ❖ Haywood Patterson
- ❖ Ozie Powell
- ❖ Victoria Price
- ❖ Willie Roberson
- ❖ Charles Weems
- ❖ Eugene Williams
- ❖ Andrew Wright
- ❖ Leroy "Roy" Wright

Highlights of Event

❖ On March 25, 1931, nine hoboing African-American young men were ordered off a train at a stop in Alabama. Two white women claimed to have been violently raped. Though there was no evidence, the men were arrested.

❖ The first trial for the nine Scottsboro Boys occurred from April 6 to April 9, 1931. In the end, eight were found guilty and sentenced to the death penalty.

❖ The Scottsboro verdict was appealed to the Alabama Supreme Court and upheld on March 24, 1932. Then, the verdict was appealed to the US Supreme Court. The court ruled that the defendants did not receive proper counsel, a retrial was set.

❖ On March 27, 1933, a new trial began. Attorney Samuel Leibowitz represented the boys. Patterson was found guilty.

❖ On June 22, 1933, the judge declared a retrial. A new trial for Patterson and Norris began on November 20, 1933. The prosecution and the judge conspired to move the jury toward a guilty verdict.

❖ The guilty verdict was again contested on the grounds that no African Americans were on the prospective jury rolls. The US Supreme Court found the Norris trial had been unconstitutional and ordered new trials for Norris and Patterson.

❖ From July 12 to July 24, 1937, the young men faced new trials. While five of the boys were found guilty, four were released.

❖ Four of the five young men still in prison were paroled. The fifth, who remained in jail, eventually escaped. Eventually, all were pardoned.

Quote

"I was convicted in [the jury's] minds before I went on trial. . . . All that spoke for me on that witness stand was my black skin—which didn't do so good."—*Patterson*

GLOSSARY

affidavit
> A written declaration under oath.

black codes
> Codes that forbade blacks from activities such as the right to serve on juries, the right to rent or own land, the right to bear arms, and even the right to read, among others.

communism
> A form of government in which industry and agriculture are owned and controlled by the state, with the ultimate goal of sharing all goods equally among the people.

cross-examination
> To question a witness called by the opposing side.

defendant
> In a trial, the person accused of a crime.

defense
> A defendant and his or her counsel.

deliberation
> The discussions held by a jury that allow it to reach a verdict.

discrimination
> Unfair treatment, often based on race, religion, or gender.

extradition
> The surrender of a criminal from one state to the other.

gondola
> A low-walled, open railroad freight car that is used to haul loads such as coal or gravel.

jury roll
> A list of people determined by a commission to be eligible for serving on a potential jury.

Ku Klux Klan
> A secret organization that aims to control and eliminate certain groups—such as African Americans, Jews, Catholics, and others—through violent, terroristic means.

lynch
> A murder by a mob, especially referring to hanging.

parole
> To release a prisoner early under specific conditions, such as being monitored or not crossing state borders.

prejudice
> Hostile, unreasonable feelings toward a person or group according to his or her race, religion, or social group.

prosecution
> The legal team working to convict a defendant.

racism
> Hatred of others because of their race.

segregationist
> Someone who believes that different groups should be kept apart according to race or ethnicity.

testify
> To make a statement on the witness stand.

white supremacist
> Someone who believes the white race is superior to all other races or ethnicities.

ADDITIONAL RESOURCES

SELECTED BIBLIOGRAPHY

Acker, James R. *Scottsboro and Its Legacy*. Westport, CT: Praeger, 2008. Print.

Carter, Dan T. *Scottsboro: a Tragedy of the American South*. Baton Rouge, LA: Louisiana State UP, 1969. Print.

Goodman, James. *Stories of Scottsboro*. New York: Pantheon, 1994. Print.

Kinshasa, Kwando Mbiassi. *The Man from Scottsboro*. Jefferson, NC: McFarland, 1997. Print.

Miller, James A. *Remembering Scottsboro*. Princeton, NJ: Princeton UP, 2009. Print.

Norris, Clarence, and Sybil Washington. *The Last of the Scottsboro Boys*. New York: Putnam, 1979. Print.

FURTHER READINGS

Kahn, Lin Shi. *Scottsboro, Alabama: A Story in Linoleum Cuts*. New York: New York UP, 2002. Print.

Web Links

To learn more about the Scottsboro Boys, visit ABDO Publishing Company online at **www.abdopublishing.com**. Web sites about the Scottsboro Boys are featured on our Book Links page. These links are routinely monitored and updated to provide the most current information available.

Places to Visit

Birmingham Civil Rights Institute
520 Sixteenth Street N.
Birmingham, AL 35203
205-328-9696
http://www.bcri.org
Many important movements in the civil rights movement occurred in or near Birmingham, Alabama. Learn about the city and the history that happened there.

The Scottsboro Boys Museum & Cultural Center
428 W. Willow Street
Scottsboro, AL 35768
256-244-1310
http://bama.ua.edu/~jaray4
This museum and cultural center commemorates the nine Scottsboro Boys and celebrates people who take a stand against racism.

The Supreme Court of the United States
1 First Street NE
Washington, DC 20543
202-479-3000
http://www.supremecourt.gov
You can tour the Supreme Court building and learn about various cases tried there.

SOURCE NOTES

Chapter 1. Segregation and Jim Crow

1. James R. Acker. *Scottsboro and Its Legacy*. Westport, CT: Praeger, 2008. Print. 3.

2. James R. Acker. *Scottsboro and Its Legacy*. Westport, CT: Praeger, 2008. Print. 3.

3. James Goodman. *Stories of Scottsboro*. New York: Pantheon, 1994. Print. 45.

4. Kwando Mbiassi Kinshasa. *The Man from Scottsboro*. Jefferson, NC: McFarland, 1997. Print. 115.

Chapter 2. The Terrible Journey Begins

1. James Goodman. *Stories of Scottsboro*. New York: Pantheon, 1994. Print. 3.

2. Kwando Mbiassi Kinshasa. *The Man from Scottsboro*. Jefferson, NC: McFarland, 1997. Print. 27.

3. Ibid. 26.

4. James Goodman. *Stories of Scottsboro*. New York: Pantheon, 1994. Print. 5.

5. Kwando Mbiassi Kinshasa. *The Man from Scottsboro*. Jefferson, NC: McFarland, 1997. Print. 38.

6. James Goodman. *Stories of Scottsboro*. New York: Pantheon, 1994. Print. 5.

Chapter 3. The Trial

1. James R. Acker. *Scottsboro and Its Legacy*. Westport, CT: Praeger, 2008. Print. 18.

2. Ibid. 18.

3. James Goodman. *Stories of Scottsboro*. New York: Pantheon, 1994. Print. 41.

4. James R. Acker. *Scottsboro and Its Legacy*. Westport, CT: Praeger, 2008. Print. 18.

5. Clarence Norris and Sybil Washington. *The Last of the Scottsboro Boys*. New York: G. P. Putnam's Sons, 1979. Print. 22.

6. Kwando Mbiassi Kinshasa. *The Man from Scottsboro*. Jefferson, NC: McFarland, 1997. Print. 40.

7. James R. Acker. *Scottsboro and Its Legacy*. Westport, CT: Praeger, 2008. Print. 22.

8. Ibid. 24.

9. James Goodman. *Stories of Scottsboro*. New York: Pantheon, 1994. Print. 97.

10. James R. Acker. *Scottsboro and Its Legacy*. Westport, CT: Praeger, 2008. Print. 24.

11. David Aretha. *The Trial of the Scottsboro Boys*. Greensboro, NC: Morgan Reynolds, 2008. Print. 39.

Chapter 4. Support for the Boys

1. James R. Acker. *Scottsboro and Its Legacy*. Westport, CT: Praeger, 2008. Print. 35.

2. James Goodman. *Stories of Scottsboro*. New York: Pantheon, 1994. Print. 84.

3. Ibid. 7.

4. Ibid. 83.

5. Ibid. 7.

6. Ibid. 84.

Chapter 5. The Supreme Court

1. James R. Acker. *Scottsboro and Its Legacy*. Westport, CT: Praeger, 2008. Print. 44.

2. James Goodman. *Stories of Scottsboro*. New York: Pantheon, 1994. Print. 112.

3. James R. Acker. *Scottsboro and Its Legacy*. Westport, CT: Praeger, 2008. Print. 50.

4. Kwando Mbiassi Kinshasa. *The Man from Scottsboro*. Jefferson, NC: McFarland, 1997. Print. 51.

5. James R. Acker. *Scottsboro and Its Legacy*. Westport, CT: Praeger, 2008. Print. 41.

SOURCE NOTES CONTINUED

Chapter 6. The Retrial

1. James Goodman. *Stories of Scottsboro*. New York: Pantheon, 1994. 121.

2. Dan T. Carter. *Scottsboro: a Tragedy of the American South*. Baton Rouge, LA: Louisiana State UP, 1969. Print. 210.

3. Ibid. 205.

4. James R. Acker. *Scottsboro and Its Legacy*. Westport, CT: Praeger, 2008. Print. 73.

5. Dan T. Carter. *Scottsboro: a Tragedy of the American South*. Baton Rouge, LA: Louisiana State UP, 1969. Print. 235.

6. James Goodman. *Stories of Scottsboro*. New York: Pantheon, 1994. Print. 211.

Chapter 7. Tried Again

1. James Goodman. *Stories of Scottsboro*. New York: Pantheon, 1994. Print. 210.

2. Dan T. Carter. *Scottsboro: a Tragedy of the American South*. Baton Rouge, LA: Louisiana State UP, 1969. Print. 244.

3. Claudia Durst Johnson. *Understand to Kill a Mockingbird*. Westport, CT: Greenwood, 1994. Print. 57.

4. James R. Acker. *Scottsboro and Its Legacy*. Westport, CT: Praeger, 2008. Print. 102.

5. Ibid. 106.

6. James Goodman. *Stories of Scottsboro*. New York: Pantheon, 1994. Print. 227.

7. James R. Acker. *Scottsboro and Its Legacy*. Westport, CT: Praeger, 2008. Print. 124.

Chapter 8. Supreme Court Justice

1. James R. Acker. *Scottsboro and Its Legacy*. Westport, CT: Praeger, 2008. Print. 141.

2. Dan T. Carter. *Scottsboro: a Tragedy of the American South*. Baton Rouge, LA: Louisiana State UP, 1969. Print. 325.

3. James Goodman. *Stories of Scottsboro*. New York: Pantheon, 1994. Print. 250.

Chapter 9. Back to Alabama

1. James R. Acker. *Scottsboro and Its Legacy*. Westport, CT: Praeger, 2008. Print. 160-161.

2. Ibid. 161.

3. Ibid. 161.

4. Ibid. 165.

Chapter 10. The Bitter End

1. Dan T. Carter. *Scottsboro: a Tragedy of the American South*. Baton Rouge, LA: Louisiana State UP, 1969. Print. 384.

2. Ibid. 385.

3. James Goodman. *Stories of Scottsboro*. New York: Pantheon, 1994. Print. 277.

4. Ibid. 275.

5. Dan T. Carter. *Scottsboro: a Tragedy of the American South*. Baton Rouge, LA: Louisiana State UP, 1969. Print. 382-383.

6. James R. Acker. *Scottsboro and Its Legacy*. Westport, CT: Praeger, 2008. Print. 193.

7. James Goodman. *Stories of Scottsboro*. New York: Pantheon, 1994. Print. 275.

INDEX

ABOUT THE AUTHOR

David Cates is an author and teacher. He has written and taught English in diverse locations around the world, such as India, Nepal, and Japan. Cates lives in Georgia with his family.

PHOTO CREDITS